BITTERING, N
LOST AND FOUND

Joan Norton's story
in her own words,
as told to Tim Cawkwell

Sforzinda Books, Norwich 2018

CONTENTS PAGE

"Lives can only be written from personal knowledge, which is growing every day less, and in a short time is lost forever. What is known can seldom be immediately told; and when it might be told it is no longer known."

Samuel Johnson, 'Lives of the Poets'

INTRODUCTION

Joan Norton likes to talk, and I like to listen to her. Her face is animated, her speech is lively, and it is delivered not just with the accent with which Norfolk English should be properly spoken, but with Norfolk-isms. Vernacular rhythms can be quite as interesting as so-called educated ones.

It may be that Joan speaks not just with a Norfolk accent, but with a Bittering accent, for it was in this tiny, isolated corner of the country that she was born in 1942 and brought up before moving to Hingham in her mid-twenties. As she told me about her early life in her characteristic voice, I was struck by how different it was to my own experience. It was perfectly believable but so difficult to imagine: compared to a comfortable middle-class upbringing, hers was a life of privation – yet she never saw it that way; to someone dwelling in a city or a suburb, it was exotically rural and remote – yet it was living in a busy, noisy town that seemed strange to her. Thirdly, Joan in a way had not one but two families, her own one living in a simple cottage, and the family living in the big house where she worked. For all these reasons I was drawn to understand more about this world that has been hidden from most people's imagination.

The account of her life in Bittering is indeed 'history from below', in the historian EP Thompson's phrase, or more exactly, it is a a story insisting that it will be told, and a voice insisting that it will be heard. I was struck at first by the idea that here was a working-class voice not from the mills and mines of the North, home of the working-class aristocracy, but from a peripheral lowland village. That might suggest the proud union of farm-workers, but Joan's early life was grittier still for it was spent in service, with no place for unions or a sense of one's own class. What is more the idea of 'the English working-class' has predominantly been a male one, which is yet another reason why Joan's voice has been less likely to be heard.

This is my attempt to rectify that. The text starts with her story as it was told to a friend who began taking it down and typing it up, but who left it unfinished. I have supplemented it with 'the story adorned'. For this I interviewed Joan over several sessions, and transcribed those interviews. However, direct speech with the words and thoughts tumbling out cannot be reproduced on the page, which is why I have edited them. What is more her mind is like a billiard ball fizzing across the green baize and continually bouncing in new directions. In editing her words I had to create some semblance of a narrative without destroying the liveliness of her train of thought.

As well as speaking to me on the record, Joan showed me and my wife Maggie round Bittering. It did not take long to see round the place – Bittering's full name is Bittering Parva (which means 'small') and it's not called that for nothing since Kelly's Directory in 1937 records the population in 1931 as being nineteen. These visits turned out to be elegiac: Joan showed us the site of Bittering Hall – demolished; Bell Hall – gone and the site overrun with trees; Wendling Airfield – now a field of corn. Looking at the map, you see traces of a long history: Salter's Lane is on the line of the old Roman road; the Launditch is an Anglo-Saxon earthwork (or is it earlier than that?); one field of bumps and hollows is the site of a mediaeval village, and across the road on a spot buried by trees is a mediaeval castle and moat. Only the parish church stands: in disrepair 100 years ago, it was re-opened in 1961, but its future as a place of worship is now in question again. And there is no more poignant sight than that of the woodland shrine built by Paul Hodác to honour his deliverance in World War Two, now enveloped by trees and wanting, in Joan's phrase, a bit of TLC.

Bittering's presence, its existence almost, seems to be slipping from our grasp. The oral historian George Ewart Evans remarks in 'Ask the Fellows Who Cut the Hay' (about the village of Blaxhall in Suffolk) that "anything that has happened within the present century is hardly worth the name of history" with the result that "the historical foreground is in many respects a blank". Just as he had his reasons for scrutinizing his particular foreground, I felt the same with the immediate past that Joan describes. It is like a framed photograph on the wall which, through exposure to time, sunlight and indifference, is fading: details are being lost, leaving only a bare outline. As it happens Bittering's present history is being made through the use of its land as a quarry for sand and gravel, and although we need sand and gravel for roads and for foundations its excavation is at Bittering's expense. Its history is not just being lost, but this injury is compounded by the gouging out of the land on which it stands.

So, this book aims to circumvent that process, at least in part. It starts with a map or two and a series of images to convey a visual flavour of this history, but the main course is definitely Joan's feast of words. I should add that in describing how Bittering's history is in its way a vanishing one is to some extent an injustice. The website, Norfolk Heritage Explorer, has a remarkable amount of information on Bittering's archaeology and on the objects found in the parish. Go to: http://www.heritage.norfolk.gov.uk/record-details?TNF220. Secondly, page 128 of the report 'The Archaeology of Norfolk's Aggregate Landscape'(produced by a joint English Heritage and Norfolk Museums and Archaeology Service project no. 5241MAIN, the National Mapping Programme) has an excellent aerial photograph online of the Little Bittering mediaeval settlement. If physical history is being lost, proper research is ensuring that the memory of it is not being lost as well.

My main thanks must go to Joan for her co-operation and the loan of personal photographs. This is very much her story, at least so far, and it is Norfolk's history – and England's too.

Tim Cawkwell / Norwich 2018

TIMELINE

1942	Joan Warmer born on 2nd October
1947	first attended Litcham School
1952	started work at Bittering Hall part-time
1957	left school and went to work full-time at the Hall
1967	in early June, Joan learns of the Napiers' plans to move to Spain which they do on 19th June. On 23rd June Joan's father committed suicide, and on 29th June her mother died.
1967	in autumn, moved to Hingham
1968	started going out with George Norton
1969	left Laurence and Scott
1973	married George
1973/4	got council house in Hingham
1982	son Brian born

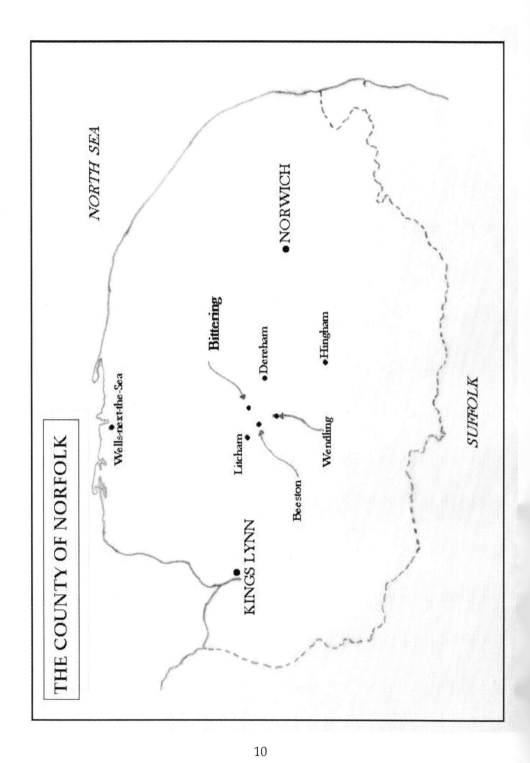

THE COUNTY OF NORFOLK

NORTH SEA

SUFFOLK

NORWICH

Bittering

Dereham

Hingham

Wells-next-the-Sea

Litcham

Wendling

Beeston

KINGS LYNN

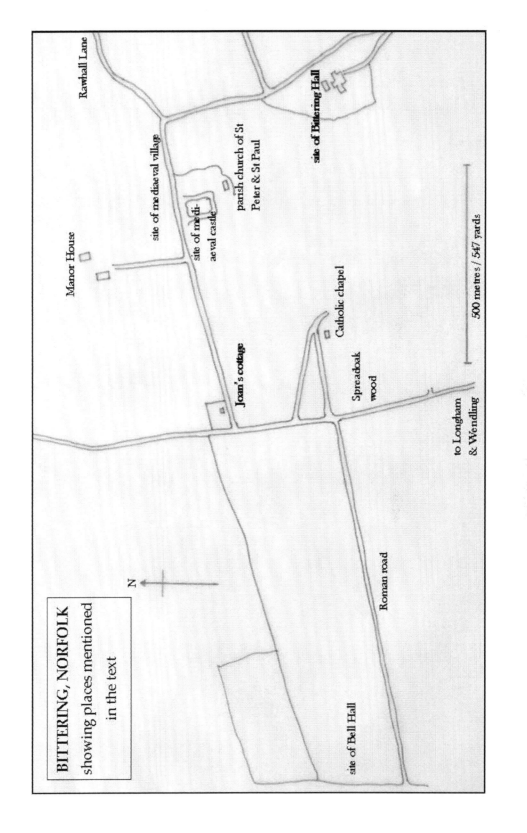

BITTERING, NORFOLK
showing places mentioned
in the text

N

Rawhall Lane

Manor House

site of mediaeval village

site of medi-
aeval castle

parish church of St
Peter & St Paul

site of Bittering Hall

Joan's cottage

Catholic chapel

Spreadoak
wood

to Longham
& Wendling

Roman road

site of Bell Hall

500 metres / 547 yards

GALLERY OF IMAGES

Joan around the age of five. The lower picture was taken when she first attended Litcham School, betraying a certain anxiety at this wider world.

Joan's siblings: Olive the eldest, born in 1928 (top), John born in 1931 (middle) and Tony the youngest, born in 1947. She also had another sister Margaret born in 1940.

above: Joan with her bicycle; below: Joan (right) and her sister
Margaret as bridesmaids.

Joan's grandparents, Charles William Warmer (1869-1924) who married Mary Ann Tooke (ca 1878-1911). They married in 1898, and at the front the photo shows Joan's father (1900-67) as a boy. It must have been taken around 1910. As a family photograph like this would have been a commonplace, they would have been bread-and-butter work for professional photographers. Nowadays it would be done with a camera phone, and purposefully informal.

In the canteen at Laurence and Scott's – Joan is in the middle at the back.

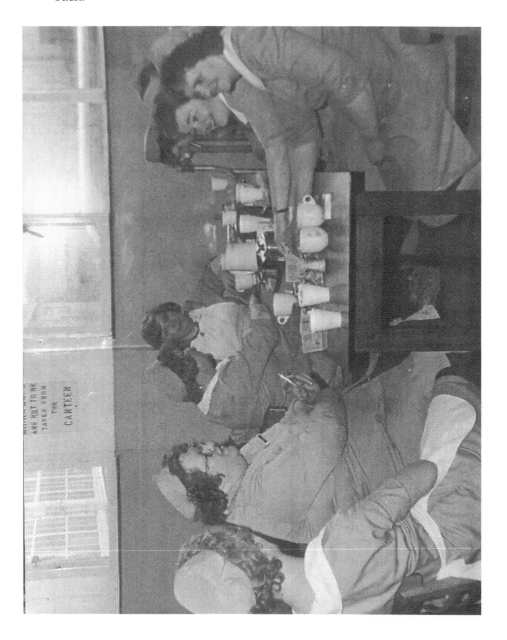

Bittering disappearing

The site of Bittering Hall in 2017; below, the tiled
floor is disappearing under grass and moss.

above: Bittering Hall; below: the drive to Bell Hall.

left: a driveway at Wendling airfield; below: Joan with Maggie Cawkwell gazing at the airfield, now a field of corn (see Annex 3).

The Roman road running through Bittering.

The long meadow (above) at Bittering which is the site of the mediaeval village. Below is a tree on the site which must have been a
seedling well after the village was sinking into the landscape.

The Catholic
chapel in Spread
Oak wood (see
Annex 1).

Easter Day Service.

Celebration and Communion

Refreshments and fellowship after the service

Sunday 27th March 2016

The Lord is Risen

The two then explained to them what had happened on the
road, and how they had recognized the Lord when he
broke the bread.

Alleluia, Christ is risen.
He is risen indeed, hallelujah.

Hymn 109 Crown him with many crowns.

Christ died to sin once for all. Let us renew our resolve to
have done with all that is evil and confess our sins in
penitence and faith.

We have lived by our own strength and not by the power of
your resurrection. In your mercy, forgive us.

Lord hear us and help us.

We have lived by the light of our own eyes, faithless and not
believing. In your mercy, forgive us.

Lord hear us and help us.

We have lived for this world alone and doubted our home in
heaven. In your mercy, forgive us.

Lord hear us and help us.

It is right to give thanks and praise.

It is indeed right.......
.........For ever praising you and saying

**Holy Holy, Holy Lord God of power and might Heaven
and earth are full of your glory.
Hosanna in the highest.
Blessed is he who comes in the name of the Lord.
Hosanna in the highest.**

Accept our praises.......
.........the memorial of Christ your
own son our Lord

Great is the mystery of faith

Christ has died, Christ is risen, Christ will come again.

Accept through him.......
.........in songs of everlasting praise

**Blessing and honour and glory and power be yours for
ever and ever. Amen.**

The Peace

*The risen Lord Jesus came and stood among the disciples
and said "peace be with you" and they were glad when they
saw the Lord.*

May the peace of the Lord be with you always
And also with you.

Let us offer each other a sign of peace.

Hymn 453 Low in the grave he lay

<u>*The Communion*</u>

**Yours Lord is the greatness, the power, the glory, the
splendour and the majesty: for everything in heaven and
on earth is yours. All things come from you and of your
own do we give you.**

The Lord is here
His spirit is with us

Lift up your hearts
We lift them to the Lord
Let us give thanks to the Lord our God

Today receive from me the water of life which I give freely to all those who ask".

First reading. Acts 10: 34-43

Choir.

Second reading. John 20:1-18

Sermon.

Hymn 988 How deep the Fathers love for us

Jesus is the very nature of God himself. He did not consider equality with God as something to be grasped but made himself nothing, taking on the very nature of a servant. Being found in appearance as a man he humbled himself and became obedient to death, even death on the cross. God then exalted him to the highest place and gave him the name that is above every name. At the name of Jesus every knee shall bow, in heaven and earth and under the earth, and every tongue will confess that Jesus Christ is Lord, to the glory of God the Father. Amen.

Prayers.

May the God of love and power, love that goes beyond and power that overcomes death forgive us and free us from our sins, heal and strengthen us by his Spirit, and raise us to new life in Christ Jesus our Lord. Amen.

Hymns 45 At your feet we fall
          795 You laid aside your majesty

Christ is behind us in all our yesterdays, he is with us in our today and before us in all our tomorrows. He is Alpha and Omega, he is Lord of all.

The Redeemer is risen, His glory fills the earth.

A trumpet sounds through all the earth, our morning star is alive.

Risen in splendour, he is among us and the darkness is driven back.

Today we are washed clean and renewed in hope. We learn how to grow together as one.
Today Jesus turns our sorrow into joy and humbles the proudest of hearts.

Jesus says "come to me all who are heavy laden and I will
give you rest

Our Father who art in heaven hallowed be thy name: thy kingdom come thy will be done on earth as it is in heaven. Give us this day our daily bread and forgive us our trespasses, as we forgive those who trespass against us. Lead us not into temptation but deliver us from evil. For thine is the kingdom the power and the glory for ever and ever. Amen.

We break this bread to share in the body of Christ

Though we are many we are one body because we all share in one bread.

Draw near with faith, receive the body of our Lord Jesus Christ which he gave for you and his blood which he shed for you.

We share in Communion.

God of life who for our redemption gave your only son to death on a cross, and by his glorious resurrection has delivered us from the power of our enemy: grant us so to die daily to sin that we may evermore live with him in the joy of his risen life, through Jesus Christ our Lord.

**Almighty God we thank you for feeding us with the body
and blood of your son Jesus Christ.
Through him we offer you our souls and bodies to be a
living sacrifice. Send us out in the power of your spirit to
live and work to your praise and glory. Amen.**

Hymn 689 Thine be the glory

Blessing

*May the Father of life pour out his grace on you, may you
feel his hand in everything you do.
May the Son of God shepherd you in all your days.*

*May his spirit comfort you and make you strong. May he
discipline you gently when you are wrong and in your heart
may he give you a song.*

Grave of Joan's parents in Bittering churchyard. It reads:

In loving memory of
JOHN WARMER
died 23rd June 1967
aged 67 years
also his wife
OLIVE
died 29th June 1967
aged 60 years
may they rest in peace

Joan was confirmed at Beeston church on Ascension Day, 19th May 1966. She had been given a Book of Common Prayer by Heather Napier's mother on her twenty-first birthday, 2nd October 1963.

Bittering church

1 THE BARE STORY

I was born Joan Warmer in 1942 In Bittering.

When I was a girl, I lived in Bittering, where my father was gardener at Bittering Hall. I went to work at the hall when I was about ten years old, in my school holidays and after school hours. When I left school at fifteen, I went there full-time. That was 1957.

Mostly I lived at home, as the cottage was only just down the road from the Hall. During the holidays I lived in the Hall as the adults went off and left me to look after the children.

My work hours were from about 9 in the morning to 4 in the afternoon, but most days, especially when the family had company, I had to go back after tea, about 7, and work through to midnight or later. This was for six days a week, but also on a Sunday if I was needed.

When I first started to work, there were other staff, but as they left they were not replaced and in the end it was only me.

My first job in the morning was to open the house, pulling the curtains and taking down the bars on the doors. Then I had to set the breakfast, and afterwards clear the table and wash up. I had to set all meals and do all the washing up. While the family had breakfast, I cleaned the smoke room. After breakfast I cleaned the rest of the house. There were twelve bedrooms, three bathrooms, and five living rooms, besides two kitchens in the washroom. Not all the bedrooms were used when just the family were home, but they all had to be gone over weekly.

I had to help cook the lunch, serve, clean and wash up. Besides the house, I also had to clean the two stable flats, which were let, and the cottage.

At that time, there were Mr and Mrs Napier at home and their son, Lenox. They were also guardians to two girls, who were also there most of the time.

I also worked at the Manor Farmhouse when I was needed. This was owned by the Napiers and used as a let, no one permanent was in that. If someone wanted to come down for a couple of years or six months, then they did.

I had to fit this in by going back evenings or afternoons – I never had no time for myself.

Mrs Napier made me churchwarden of Bittering church so that I could go clean up in the church so that it was always in good order for the services once a month. I did not get paid for this.

When I first went as a schoolgirl, I used to get fifteen shillings (75p) per week. That was from nine o'clock in the morning on a Saturday until they didn't want me no more. It might be at four o'clock, but then I might go across to clean the flat. I never knew when I was wanted. Being in a tied cottage you was always at their beck and call. I'd never go into a tied cottage no more, your life isn't your own, you're just used.

When I went full time I got £1 10s. (£1.50) per week. When I left in June 1967, I was getting £5 10s. (£5.50) per week. I was 25 years old then. [Note: since in 1967 Joan was working 42 hours a week – and there were plenty of unpaid hours on top of that – this is equivalent to £2.32 an hour in 2018, which is not a great purchasing power.]

Dad was never very well, but started getting bad in 1966 and died in 1967. Mum went into hospital in 1964 and when she came out they said she had only two to three years to live, but could drop down dead anyway. From then on, I looked after them as well as working. My youngest brother, Tony, was at home too.

Our cottage had no water and we had to get water from the old pit hole in the garden. We used to have to go down with a bucket and a hand cup and fill the buckets and take them to the wash-house. For drinking, our water come from the well just down the road about 150 yards away. You had to wind a bucket down and then pour it into another bucket and carry it home. If the well went dry, we had to go to the Manor Farm for drinking water with a milk churn on a pram. All the washing or bathwater was boiled in the coppers, one outside and one in the wash-house. You couldn't save enough rainwater to go through the summer although we had big rainwater tanks, and we used to look after them like gold dust. We would rush with a bucket if rainwater was coming off a roof and catch it.

I left the cottage in 1967 after father and mother died but I paid the rent several years so they could not turn me out if I wanted to go back.

Mrs Napier learned to me to do things her way, like moving all furniture and dusting the skirting boards. If she told you to do a room she would expect you to move everything and do it properly. No matter how big or small, the furniture had to be moved. She told me how to move furniture and that like. All rooms now are so small there's not room to move the furniture so I find it difficult to do the room. Mrs Napier had been in charge of something in the war – I wondered if she had been a matron, she was that kind of person. Someone said she's a nice lady but a proper old ma'am of the old school. I got on all right with her and they treated me as one of the family, but life was just hard and difficult.

If they went out, they took me as well to the cinema or anywhere. The biggest break I had was going to church – at least I could sit down. When they said, 'All stand', I used to sit down, glad of a rest.

There's only eight hours in a working day but there's twenty-four hours in the day and I worked a lot more than eight hours. The Napiers did a lot of entertaining. Sometimes I would leave off at two in the morning, go home and then be up again at seven to get Tony off to work. Then I would make sure the fires were made up under the coppers and in the front room, and that there was plenty of water, and that Mum and Dad were all right, and then be at the Hall by nine o'clock. Dad had his bed in the front room. We had to wash up on the table there. There was no sink we just had bowls. I made sure their breakfasts and dinners were ready before I went. If I could I liked to come off home at dinner time to make sure that everything was okay.

***

After the Napiers went to Spain in 1967 and I had left the Hall, Dad committed suicide on the Friday and then the following Friday, Mum died. Dad had only four weeks to live anyway.

28

2   THE STORY ADORNED: CHILDHOOD

Money in the hedgerow and food on the table

Joan: Dad was a market gardener, and he used to get things from the land to sell.

Tim: Can you remember what things you got from Litcham Common as a family?

J: Meadowsweet. Stinging nettles. Then come the horseradish.

Wild horse radish had stems in the ground, like carrot stems. That used to stink. You can smell that a mile off. You dig them up, cut the long shoots off at the bottom, the little shoots you leave on and put them back in the hole with the top and then they'll grow again. And then you cut them off the next time.

There was silicon spiders 'cos we had to get the cobwebs. They are very small spiders and they make silicon cotton. You used to have to get that. And then there was wild sage. Anything wild what he could sell, you see. There were quite a lot of money on Litcham Common that we used to get.

He used to sell things to big hotels up in London. The horseradish was to make horseradish sauce. Some of what we got used to go to laboratories. Meadowsweet used to go there and stinging nettles. There's two things you can make out of stinging nettles. One you make aspirins with, I know that one. From the other one you make toilet paper. Years ago we never had soft toilet paper; that was like grease-proof paper.

Dad always used to take us out. Mum said, what was true, we had to go through either ditches or go through blooming brambles. We never go out for a walk on the road because we didn't. That wasn't Dad. If he could find something that he could sell that was a lot better than anything.

T: Did you get mushrooms?

J: Plenty of mushrooms, on the long meadow just round there by the cottage opposite the parish church [and site of the mediaeval village]. It had never been ploughed up.

And you can eat some toadstools.

T: If you know what you're eating.

J: He did. He knew. And we also got wild watercress growing in the long meadow. Also chestnuts at wintertime. We never had to buy them, we got them from the wood. Wood nuts. Walnuts. Anything what we could eat and get free, we got. I mean the gypsies like going in the wood to get chestnuts. They used to go on Swaffham Market. They'd make a little cone with paper, and then put roast chestnuts in. About half a crown, they cost. They didn't have to buy the chestnuts because God created them in the wood. All they had to do was to go out and pick them.

And we used to get some dandelions, for dandelion burdock. That was sort of like a drink. If you had a cold that was good for you.

Dad was a very clever man really. What he done was all what God provided for us. There was nothing he actually grew himself. I know he used to sell trees. Honestly speaking, he really and truly got as much as he could from the hedgerows.

Mum used to make sugarbeet bread because that's the only thing you can make out of sugarbeet. You can't really make sugar. When I worked at Laurence and Scott, they said, 'You bring the sugarbeet in and put it in our tea.' I said, 'You won't drink it, that's horrible.' That may be sugarbeet but it hent what you think.

T: The sugarbeet bread can't have been very nice.

J: If you're hungry you eat it, don't you? But we never went hungry. But Mum didn't have much in the pantry.

T: When you went to school did you go to the shop and get things after school?

J: We went to the shop across the road before we went to school.

When we come out of school we used to get ice lollies.

T: How old were you when you ate your first bowl of cornflakes?

J: I can't remember. When you start eating cornflakes you start eating properly.

*

The shop is five miles from Bittering, you wouldn't walk there every day. And on the way you've got that hill. I got hit when we were pushing the barrow up the hill. We nearly got up to the top, and this car came out the gate and hit the wheelbarrow. They must've heard us because we weren't quiet kids, I can assure you. We could make all the noise we liked because we weren't disturbing anybody. I mean you are sort of miles away from anywhere.

T: How old are you? Were you badly injured?

J: I must've been about five or six. I had a bloody nose and Mum was a-shouting because she was walking up the road with Tony on the back of her bike, and Dad was miles in front, as usual, and we was pushing the barrow up the hill, and this car just come out.

*

When the fog come round and spiders make webs, sort of like silicon, we used to have to go and pick all that so he could send it away. That used to go to a laboratory.

We used to have to go to Wells to get a load of seaweed to send away to laboratories.

T: He got money for it?

J: He would take us there on the cart, break at Wells Woods and have a cup of tea because we always used to take a little stove and we'd have a cup of tea and a break like. We used to go on to Wells and collect a lot of seaweed up because that make iodine, and different things. We got money for it.

And in the midst of this he used to plant things in the hedgerows for the gypsies, like gooseberry bushes and all sorts of different apple trees, so that they could eat them or sell them. That was the man he was. He didn't just think about us having food. Really and truly living round there you didn't have to buy anything. There were plenty of rabbits, plenty of hares, plenty of pheasants. There's all sorts around there. Of course we used to go poaching. We used to go down to the river Bilney way.

T: What were you poaching?

J: We used to go poaching fish. Trout, anything like that.

T: And how do you catch them?

J: He catch 'em with his hands.

T: He would stand in the water, would he?

J: Yes.

T: That took some patience, I would think.

J: He could just get them like that and hit them at the side of the head. Sometimes he just bring them home alive. You get them in a bucket and we used to come off home with them.

You see, when you live out in the countryside like we did, you couldn't have a gun because you'd be caught if the gun go off! That sound a lot louder than them things going off what frighten the birds, because there is no one there, is there? I mean if that's going off in Norwich say, you wouldn't hardly hear it because of all the other noise there.

You catch pheasants and that by putting a net round, and getting behind them so they'll fly into the net.

Helping father at harvest

J: That's an old-fashioned way of doing things. You stand the sheaf up like this. Right. You get about six or eight in a thing. And then the tractor come around and pick them up and go on top of the trailer, and then that go through a troshing engine and then that go up into a stack.

T: So what was your job?

J: I used to help my Dad at night time. Some nights we used to go out on the field. I used to help him stack them up. I used to pick them up and then hand them to him and he'd go and put 'em like that because they'd got to stand up properly.

T: That's a sheaf of wheat? Quite heavy, I should think.

J: Well, they aren't light, are they?

T: So what age were you doing that?

J: I was at school when I'd done that. 11 or 12 years old.

T: You must've been strong.

J: You never took any notice. That's like when the well used to go dry. You'd have to go and put a milk churn on top of a pram and go and fill it up with water away from the farm. Then you'd put it off home, so you'd have your cups of tea and the like. Life wasn't easy round there, but it was a way of life.

Joan's siblings

[Olive was born in 1928, married Geoffrey Blake; John was born in 1931, married Pat Girling; Margaret was born in 1940, married Laurence Chappell; Joan was born in 1942, married George Norton; Tony was born in 1947, married Gloria Raper]

J: My younger brother Tony used to come up the Hall to play with Lenox [Napier]. Even though there was a big age difference it didn't seem to matter. They used to take Tony out to the seaside. In a way he had the best out of all of us, from Margaret, Johnny, Olive and me. The five of us. He was the one who had the best bit because they took him around. If they went out for a meal or anything, Tony used to go along with them. He had this fine family life being with them. I mean people used to say to me, Tony is a complete little gentleman, and I thought he'd better be! [Laughs] If not, that would have made it worse for me. I said to him, you make sure you behave yourself, they know I'm your sister. I was always afraid someone would put a spoke in, and put him into care because Mum and Dad were both in hospital. I didn't mind being in Bittering on my own. It never did worry me.

Religion

T: Did your mother and father go to chapel?

J: That wasn't till Canon Dodson came that we had a church service there in Bittering.

T: When did Canon Dodson come?

J: Canon Dodson came to Gressenhall [in 1953], and Bittering was part of that group. He reopened the church in Bittering [in 1961].

T: So, you didn't have a chapel?

J: No. Well we did at Longham, and we went to Longham Sunday School. Sometimes we used to go to Longham church, and sometimes we used to go more into the village and go into the chapel. But that way, you're more away from Longham really.

T: You might say if you'd had a car you'd jump in the car. But you didn't have a car?

J: No. Johnny did but he was a bit older. All we had was the bicycle with the trailer behind, and Dad used to take us out.

T: How many children could fit in the trailer?

J: There was just the three youngest, Margaret, me and Tony. We used to go to Wells, sitting in the back of the cart.

T: That's almost twenty miles. Your father bicycled all the way?

J: There weren't no rail station, you see.

T: Nowadays it would be a bit dangerous with all the cars but I presume the roads were fairly clear.

J: There weren't the traffic.

T: So, your Mum didn't come to Wells?

J: Yes she went as well, on her own bike. She used to have Tony on behind her sometimes, so me and Margaret was in the trailer.

T: Did you like travelling in the trailer?

J: Well, yes.

T: It was a bit bouncy, I should think!

J: You don't really think about it. We used to get as far as the woods, and used to have a run around in there. And Dad had a rest. And then we go to Wells and pick up the seaweed and cockles and that.

T: And that would be an all-day expedition?

J: Yes. Because sometimes the tide was in and we used to have to wait till that go out a bit so we could pick up the seaweed. That make iodine, you see, and different things. That's free, isn't it? I mean God made the seaweed, do you see what I mean? When I said we were brought up on God's creation, because we were, God made the sea-weed, so we collected up the seaweed, we got money for that. You say to people we had to go to Wells to pick up a lot of seaweed. They think you're barmy, there's no money in the seaweed, but there is.

*

T: Were your mother and father C of E?

J: Yes, definitely. Dad sort of loved Bittering church. That's where he lay, as you know. My mother did as well. They lived at Bittering all their lives so when they got married, they stayed there till the day they died, and they're still there.

T: So you went to Longham Sunday School, and you went to the parish church when Canon Dodson opened it. When we knew you in the 1980s, you looked after the chapel in Hingham in Chapel Street.

J: Yes. The reason I done that, it was falling down, and it's some-thing I had been used to – what shall I say? – I wasn't used to decent buildings. [Laughs]

T: I thought the chapel in Chapel Street was a lovely little building inside. The woodwork is all quality stuff.

J: They've turned it into a house now, or they are going to. I think that's sad when these places do get turned into a house. I'm glad in one sense that they're not demolished. It's the same with that church at Bittering, not the parish church but the one in the wood (see page 66). You'd think that the Catholic people would come and do something.

T: It's falling down, is it not?

J: That hent down in itself, but that do want a lot of TLC. I mean, I noticed that when we went. The side there, the ceiling is fell in. That's the state of repair. I mean that's a lovely little church. I know it only holds fourteen people. I took a neighbour back there and she got quite upset. She did try to get the Bishop at the Catholic Church, right up high, and they said that was in Longham wood, not Bittering wood. I said to her, that always has been in Bittering wood.

T: The Catholics think you should come to the small town, or to Norwich. It's my understanding that they don't spend money on buildings in lots of little places.

J: That's so heart-breaking when you go back, especially for me. When I go back to Bittering, there's always something else gone. Every time. When that man used to live there, the man who built it, his bungalow isn't there anymore.

T: When you say 'man' do you mean the Czechoslovak, Paul Hodác?

J: Yes.

T: Did you know him?

J: Yes. Because he used to have to come to our well to take the water off home to his bungalow. So he used to bring us tea and sugar and that, like, because we allowed him to use the well, but you see the well was there for everybody, there for the gypsies, there for everybody. It wasn't there just for us and for Mrs Purple next door. But for everybody.

Gypsies

T: Did gypsies come every season?

J: A lot of them used to stay all the year, and the children were born there. They went to Litcham School. Some of them went to Beeston, and in a way they stayed around there. Some of them went into council houses there at Beeston because once they give up the travelling community and go in the council house they can't go back to the travelling community.

T: And you played with the children?

J: We got called names because we were playing with them. But then you see that's racist. People was racist towards the gypsies. It's still the same.

T: You mean the people in Bittering didn't like to associate with the gypsies?

J: The Bittering people were all right, that was the Longham people.

T: But you played with the children and your Dad didn't say you mustn't do that?

J: No. They're children, aren't they? You might say, all you foreigners over that side, and we're over here. But you throw a ball or something over that side, and then they jump over the wall to play with each other. You can't get children not to. And that isn't right, they should be able to. At the same time we were called gyppos and all sorts because we played with the children.

T: Who called you that?

J: At school.

T: Did that annoy you?

J: It did. It upset me a lot, and it still do because they were with 'em as much as what we were when we were all in the school playground. You cannot put a barrier up between children. The more you try, they're there.

T: I think it's interesting that the gypsies were in Bittering but people in Bittering accepted it from what you're saying, and it was the people in the neighbouring villages who thought it was wrong because they didn't meet them, they saw less of them.

J: No, they didn't see them a lot, no.

The gypsies used to have a flag. You used to know the gypsies by the flag but they don't have it today. If the gypsies go back to how we know them, if they had the flag flying from the caravan, you knew they were gypsies. That's blue at the top, green at the bottom, and then they have a round wheel but they don't join up, as bits of spikes come out so that is their wheel in the middle of the flag but they don't join up. As far as you're concerned, that was just a wheel. They also had what we used to call the Queen's flag, the Union Jack, and that was flown as well as their flag. We always used to call that the Queen's flag, or the King's flag.

They didn't have one flag on there the other night, the gypsies' flag, and I was so angry.

T: Where was this?

J: On the television. If they had the flag, you would then know they are gypsies, not New Day Travellers.

They had their way of life. In a way I feel sorry for them in some respect because they had it hard when we were kids. That seem they have it a damn sight harder now. I mean they got fined because the children don't go to school but they can't let them go to school because they don't know when they're going to next be evicted. They hent got nowhere to go half the time.

I upset the parish council. When they put them flats up there in Hingham for the older people – I hent saying we don't need them because we do, those who want them – I said they could have put a nice big gypsy site there with bathrooms and toilets.

T: I don't suppose that went down very well.

J: It didn't! I'm always upsetting the council. When they put that site down near Norwich Road, the man was there mobbing because they were going to build houses on it. I said, "What about putting a gypsy site on there. What would you say about that? Considering gypsies hent got nowhere to go, that would make a lovely big site for the gypsies." They'd probably get about 200 caravans on there. And they could. Providing they're proper gypsies, flying their own flag.

T: Do you think they might be more tolerated if they were recognised as proper gypsies?

J: Yes, like they used to be. You see, when some of the gypsies used to come, we used to call them tinkers. They had a bell and they knew they weren't proper gypsies, so they said, "You've got to go."

T: They didn't get along with the gypsies?

J: No. That's ever so complicated.

T: What did you think about that camp near Calais in France, where the Africans had come and they wanted to come to the UK but couldn't? Did you think we should have taken them all, or more than we did?

J: I said to myself that all the governments, all over the world, should get all countries back together, even if they put up wooden cabins for them to live in in their own countries. I think we should give them money, and not just us but their own country too, so they can go back home and live in their own country because they've got the ground. I hent saying it's going to be easy. I said this in church once, on a Wednesday morning, I said, "What I would like to see is all the governments and all the church leaders, all the high and mighties, get altogether, the whole lot, and say that they would try to start re-building that country back up again." Migrants must feel strange in France or even here.

T: They are often fleeing civil war.

J: You take the Second World War. Places got bombed, but they rebuilt them. There was peace over there, so they could start rebuilding. We should all help.

T: So what do you think of Donald Trump?

J: I wish he hadn't got in. He wants to build that wall up. We got rid of the Berlin Wall, and now he wants to put the Wall back.

T: We are back to gypsies in a way. There are a lot of Mexicans in America, but they work hard and they do a lot of jobs that other people won't do. America is a huge country. They've got the space for them.

J: It's the same with the Indians, the native Americans, Indians going to Parliament in America protesting that government was taking their lands. I said to Dad, "Why do they want to treat Indians like that?" He said, "Hard to explain, that's just the way they are." But I couldn't understand why they wanted to take away their bit of land. It's their way of life. We need to live and let live.

If everyone got the attitude I got, there would be no trouble!

School, and getting around Bittering

There was too many children in the class at school. I always remember getting knocked off a chair. There was a shelf with three or four of us sitting there. Well I was only little, and I had to climb up on this here stool to sit there. And I got knocked off by the boy what brought the register.

T: They were very short of space, were they?

J: Yeah. Half the time I never did have a desk at school. Lot of them did, but I didn't. I sort of seem always to be pushed around. I even had to sit up the teacher's desk. The classes were big, even in that day, I should say at least thirty children in the class. There was some of them what had desks but I never did.

It wasn't all bad. We did nature study on Litcham Common. I used to like that.

Another thing is getting to school. If you live out there, they aren't going to come and see why you aren't at school like they do elsewhere.

T: How did you travel the five miles to school?

J: You had to walk across the fields, and we used to walk across through the wood if that was a nice day, and then go to Bell Hall, and then Mrs Andrews got us in the car and we used to go up to Beeston Road to go to school in Litcham by bus.

T: Did she bring you back?

J: She came and picked us up.

T: What happened if it was raining?

J: Because we used to have to go across the fields, we didn't bother to go to school.

T: Did that happen very often?

J: [laughs] Yes. That's muddy across the fields.

T: They get very fussed about children not being at school now, don't they? Were they more lenient then?

J: They didn't bother, not when we were there. They didn't seem to. You're miles away from anywhere. I always say you want Dr Who's Tardis. You go up in the air and land where you want!

If you hent got a car, and you rely on the bicycle you just can't go where you can't get back to. Not only that, there hent no street lighting either.

You're out in the sticks all the time. We did start going to the youth club there at Longham. You see, you've got to walk from Bittering to Longham, and that's not easy at night time, but I never did used to mind because if you went say to Beetley you often found the moon used to follow you off home. So you always had the moonlight but you don't realise just how much light there is from the moon, because we've got street lighting now, hent we? So you don't really get the effect from the moon, not really.

T: There were much fewer cars then. But did you get cars driving there at night?

41

J: Not really. Every now and again they used to have a sort of rally come round there, but not very often. I don't know why they had
the rally because the roads really and truly hent fit for having rallies.

*

We did have telly. Dad got some 12-volt car batteries and a generator
and a charger. You'd have to charge up the car batteries down the bottom of the garden, and you can run a television off that, and also you
can run an electric iron. You have one plug, and one electric light bulb,
because you can't have electric all over the place. They did down at
the farm because there's a bigger generator. Of course we were there
at the cottage and we didn't have that. We seen the first episode of
Coronation Street. So in a way we didn't go without. Our lives was so
much different.

T: When did the electricity come properly?

J: Before Mum and Dad died, about 1965. We only had it two year
down there because in 1967 I come to Hingham. We didn't really and
truly have the benefit of electricity.

T: Did you spend a very short time in the cottage in Bittering on
your own?

J: I did do when Mum and Dad were both in hospital. I took Tony
to work with me. That's another thing, you see. We were like a family.
When someone went into hospital, you always knew you'd get a pair
of pyjamas up there at Bittering Hall. There's no shops! You went up
there and they would give them to you, even though they went
without. When Dad went into hospital, I said to them he hadn't got
any pyjamas. Mr Napier said, "That's all right. I'll give him a pair of
mine and a dressing gown." You never went short because they were
always there.

[Joan shows me linen in a cupboard]

You see that lot there. They're all bedlinen what Mr and Mrs Harding
used to bring Mrs Napier when they come down. They had a factory
or something in Yorkshire and when they used to come they bring her

a load of stuff, and me the same. I used to give a bundle to Pat and Johnny, the same with towels, all brand new. Every time they came down they treated me like they did the Napiers. I never went short for anything.

Tenancies

[The family lived in the front room of their cottage. It had three bedrooms with the long bedroom at the back over the coal house. There was a small 'walk-through' kitchen with an old wall oven, an old copper, a fire, a table, and after the electricity came, a fridge. The toilet was outside the back door, and the bathroom was in the coal shed along with the copper, making it the warmest room. The house was "clean, but a bit drafty".]

T: Did your Dad have to pay rent?

J: We only paid £16 a year, that is six shillings a week. That weren't bad. [£16 is equivalent to £284 in 2018.]

T: How many tenants did the Hall have?

J: There was one in the Hall, one in the flat, one in the cottage, and one down the Manor House. Four in all. But Reggie Purple the cow-man next door and where we live, we went with the farm, and where Mrs Pooley live that also went with the farm. But even though they owned the whole lot that still went with the farm. That's all a bit complicated.

T: And the Napiers had farmland?

J: No end of farms. Quite a big farm. Them down round the Stanfield Road where I said they lived across the fields, well they bought them off the Napiers, and when the Napiers went to Spain they had the offer. I did too. I could have bought the two cottages for £500. But you see who would want to live there? At that time, you don't really think straight. The cottages were in a bad state. They had to have new troughings all the way around, and that's only the start of it. New windows. New doors. Troughings – that's Norfolk ! [Laughs] There was a lot wanting doing, and you really want the two knocked into

43

one to make it decent because the kitchen weren't very big. They have done that now.

I think when we wanted a new back door, they wouldn't put one on, so Dad done the back door with cardboard. He put it on both sides of the door, and painted over the cardboard. Keep the draught out! I'll tell you one thing we used to do when that was wintertime, the draft used to come through the windows, so we used to get some snow and make little bricks to keep the draft out. When I had my old door in this council house [in Hingham], I done that because that used to let the draft in terrible. And when that snow when Georgie and I were here, I said I might make a blooming snow thing by the front door, and he said that will be warm then. And you'd be surprised how much heat there is in snow.

I know once we couldn't get down to the well because we didn't know where the well was. We had to scrape all the snow off, then use the other bit to make up some tea. It's a wonder I'm still alive really!

I never took any harm, never have, always sort of like managed.We had a good life really. And I'm not saying it was easy round there. It wasn't.

WORKING FOR THE NAPIERS

T: How many years did you work for Mrs Napier?

J: I went there full time when I was 15 and I left there when I was 25.

T: It's hard not having any holiday.

J: Mrs Napier used to take me with her to Aylsham market. I re-member her saying, "Joan! Joan! are you keeping up?"

The thing on it is, her generation was jealous of me working for her. They couldn't get anybody, you see. Of course she got me. I'm not praising myself up, but I thought that she was put on sometimes because she had got me there.

I got on well with her and Mrs Napier's mother, Mrs McLaren. And with her sister. Like I said, we were all there together.

Like I said, they weren't good payers, I must agree. I can't say they were. But then a lot of the time, they didn't know what I was doing or nothing; I never used to tell 'em. They were good at letting me go off home for dinner times. They never did grumble. They knew how things were at home and they accepted it. You've got to give and take, haven't you?

In a way I had a good relationship with Mrs Napier. She learnt me a lot. Being the old type, she was more stricter and that, and you got in her way of doing things. Right up to today I never cut corners because I know I would never have been able to cut corners with her. She learned me to cook, she learned me how to iron properly. Everything I do is her way. In a way she learned me that money wasn't everything. There's kindness, generosity, and people are more important than money.

*

T: When they went on holiday, they didn't take you. Did you have to look after everything?

J: Yes, bad tenants and all, if they were there. The best thing to do was to be friendly with them because you kept an eye on them more if you were friendly than if you turn your back on them.

Another thing I used to do every now and again when the Napiers were away on holiday, I used to have to collect the rent money. I didn't mind doing it. That wasn't a lot of money then, so I used to put it in a plastic bag and put it in my knickers for safekeeping. If it went in the mud, it would all be in a muddle! [Laughs] Sometimes I had to take wood money out to Mr Codling, a man at Longham who used to sell wood and that like. And sometimes the tenants used to buy wood off on him. I used to say to them, I'm going that way and do you want me to take his money.

T: And they trusted you?

J: They could do nothing else, could they? I was always around.

When we had trouble off the Hall because we had some bad tenants there, the Hardings were there then. There's me working like mad trying to get the flat in some respectable state. Mrs Harding said, "Well you started everywhere, and you finished nowhere." I tried to get all the muck out. I'll never forget that, it was just horrendous, I've never known anything like it. Well the tenants were some pigs they were. That is when, I think, the Napiers thought they had had enough of this.

T: You mean that is when they thought they did not want to be bothered with tenants?

J: Yes, we had one or two lots of bad tenants. I tried to clean up. There was a time there when I was cleaning up the Hall, that is the main hall, the flat, the stable flat, the cottage, and around the house, besides the home. That was really getting on top of me. My brother John used to say I was the slave around there because it was so much work. And then there's the church. I was the churchwarden there a little while, unpaid. [Laughs] You see, all the years I worked for Mrs Napier I only had one week's holiday. And I never had a week's holiday away from Bittering.

I used to sometimes be working all day there, and I'd probably go off home for half an hour or so, and then I was back again working to goodness knows what time. 11 o'clock some nights. Sometimes it was four o'clock in the morning before I got home. I was clearing up the dishes, and everything. But I never did mind. I never did grumble. I used to just get on with it.

T: When you're young, that's how you expect the world to be?

J: I expect so.

The Napiers' move to Spain

I'd worked full-time for the Napiers for more than nine years when they broke the bad news. One Friday I was busy ironing when Mrs Napier said, "We're going away on the Monday." "Oh" I said, "that's good," because I thought they were going on holiday. "How long for?" She said, "For good." I said, "You can't go for good!" She said, "We are. Come in on Monday please and make sure you clean all up and do and when you finish, put the key in one of the flat doors." I asked for a reference and she gave me one in the finish, and £15 redundancy. She said there were no need for a reference because I was going to work round there and everybody knew me, but I said, "I'm not stopping either." She said, "What do you mean?" I said, "I'm going to work for Laurence and Scott [in Norwich] in October." She said, "You can't leave round here." "Yes I can," I said, "and I'll pay you four years' rent in advance" – that was £16 a year, paid at Michaelmas – "then I'll see if I want the cottage after four years." She said okay.

*

You see, another thing, if they had taken me over there to Spain, so I can have a look where I was going to live, say tomorrow and come back Monday, I didn't do it 'cos I hadn't got a clue about what I was going into. That was too much in the unknown. Considering it was nothing to just get in the car and go, I still couldn't do it.

I think the Napiers done the wisest thing when they went to Spain, but you don't think on it at the time.

T: You were sorry to see them go?

J: Yes. Apparently I did try to talk to them about staying. What I wanted them to do – I know you can't tell people what to do – but the way I looked at it, she was down there, they were my family, we used to talk like a family, and I said to them, why don't you go after August. Let Lenox come off home because he was working hard at his boarding school because of his exams, and I didn't think that was right that when he come away from school after working hard that he would no longer come back to Bittering, that he would be going to Spain, getting on the plane all the way to Spain to his new home. I didn't think that was right that a child should know by post that when he come out of school he was going home to Spain and not come back

47

to Bittering. Because he was born at Bittering Hall, he grew up there, and all he had was us, and all we had was him. Then all of a sudden there was this big gap between Spain and Bittering, do you see what I mean?

CRISIS

When Joan lost her job at the Hall because the Napiers moved to Spain in 1967, she was without a job, and at the same time her mother and father died.

T: When did your Mum and Dad die?

J: In 1967, in a week of each other. When Mum went into hospital to have an operation on her stomach, they said to me, "We've cleaned her up inside but we can't do anything for her. She's got cancer, you know." That was about two or four years before she died. She didn't really look after herself, like she should have done. We were so far away from the doctor's at Litcham, that's one thing.

Dad committed suicide. He was done, really. What happened was, I finished work at the Napiers on 18th/19th June. When I left Bittering Hall, Mrs Napier said, "You won't want a reference, will you?" So I said, "Yes I will because it's got to last me the rest of my life." I hent chucked it out. It's got 'Bittering Hall' on it, you see. This is the reference she give me.

T: That's from Mrs Napier?

J: Her proper name was Rosemary Heather Napier, but she always went on Heather Napier. That's 1967, Monday 19th June. When I went about getting a council house, I had to take it in. It's been quite handy all my life. That's the only bit of proof I got that I worked at Bittering Hall.

T: [reading out] "Hard-working, honest and reliable." I'll agree with that.

J: It has got a Bittering Hall heading. You can't forge that whatever happens.

Really and truly, I never ever wanted to leave Bittering. Mum and Dad put in for a council house but I wasn't going. I was going to stay down there because I worked there at the Hall, obviously. And that's where I was going to stay, but that didn't turn out like that because – well, Mrs Matthews there at Longham Hall, the Old Rectory, she was a bit of a pain. She would never take no for an answer. When Dad died on a Friday, she said, "You can come with me on Wednesday and Thursday [of the following week, 28th/29th June] to the Royal Norfolk Show." And I said that I didn't want to go because Mum was dying, she could die very soon. The police were very good, they stood their ground towards Mrs Matthews and said no, she's not going.

T: How were the police involved?

J: Because Dad committed suicide. He shot himself in the head. I was at home on my own when I found him in the garden.

T: It must've been a terrible thing to find your Dad dead in the garden.

J: I got up the Friday morning. He wasn't in bed. I thought he'd gone to the toilet 'cos the toilet was outside. I thought, I don't know, he's a bloody long while coming in. I went out there and he wasn't in the toilet. I thought where the hell is he? He must be down the bottom of the garden, and then I couldn't find him where he would be, and I came up the other way and of course I found him outside the caravan.

T: And the gun beside him?

J: Well now, the gun was in the hedge. You see, we had a big tall hedge between us and the neighbour. I told the police on the phone there were no gun, I couldn't see a gun anywhere. When they came, they said that as he shot himself, that flew up and the barrel went down that way because with the wind blowing that moved the barrel down. By the time they came I had found the gun. I didn't touch it obviously, but I did find the gun in the hedge. A little bit more and that would have gone over into Reggie Purple's garden next door.

T: That must have been awful.

J: Well, it was a long while before I could talk about it. But then people said what he done killed Mum. I said no, Mum was going to die before him anyhow. I'm glad I went to see Uncle Bob because I told him to go round and tell everybody that Mum was going to die after the Norfolk Show. That is what she done. I wanted the family to know that. It was a good job I did 'cos they couldn't say what he done kill her.

T: Do you think your Dad committed suicide because he was in tremendous pain? And he didn't want to be on his own without his wife?

J: He was very very ill. He was in a lot of pain and he knew Mum wasn't going to be about there much longer and, like I said, I don't think he really wanted the upheaval of going into the council house in Hingham, even though he was looking forward to it because that was next door to his sister. Mum and Dad lived down at Bittering all their married life. When they first got married, they went down there. And they lived there all the way through the Second World War and every-thing.

At the same time he didn't like the thought of me being down at Bit-tering on my own, what was my own choice, and I said I don't want to leave Bittering. I said I'll go on the council list, for a council house. I did for Longham, but I also put Hingham. You see the houses were built in groups of eight, in different parishes. Longham was the last one that got the eight bungalows. We knew they were going to be built but we didn't know when. Of course I was here in Hingham well before they were built. To be honest, I would rather have this bunga-low than what I would them at Longham. But then if I'd got one at Longham I wouldn't know about these ones!

I had to come and live in Hingham for five years before I got a council house. I was in Hingham six and a half years before I got this house. So because Longham was on the list, I was going to live next door to my godmother Edy Page in Longham but she was in the same situa-tion as me. She went to live along with her brother for two and a half years till the council houses were built, and then she went back to

Longham to live in her bungalow. I could have done the same, but by now, I was working at Norwich and had met Georgie. Then Hingham became my home.

T: You put yourself down for a council house at Longham and Hingham.

J: For a bungalow for myself but Mum put a council house down for herself, but when they were going to get their council house I wasn't going with them. I was going to stay down there at Bittering and keep the house on, and then I was going to sleep at the Hall. This was the whole idea of it because I said I wasn't going to bike in the early hours of the morning to where Mum and Dad live. That's the reason why Mum and Dad turned the cottage over to my name. You see, that way they knew I was alright. But I couldn't get through to Mum that I wasn't going to go into a council house with her, I was going to stay in Bittering. That was where my work was. I wasn't going to bike miles to go off home to them and then come back again 'cos as soon as I got off home I might as well come back anyhow.

T: Was there any prospect that you might sleep in the Hall?

J: I'd rather have the cottage so I could go back there and get away from it because if not I'd be working all the while. I mean, the Napiers were good because they let me turn the cottage over into my name while Mum and Dad were still alive. Therefore there were no friction there whatsoever, if you know what I mean.

*

What happened was, I left the Napiers on the Monday because they went to Spain on a Monday, and then on Friday Dad committed suicide, and then the following Thursday Mum died. We knew she was going to die after the Royal Norfolk Show, but everything happened all at once. Of course, I didn't want to leave Bittering. I did go and live with my sister Margaret in Beeston for a short time but Mrs Matthews [at Longham Hall] would never take no as an answer. I did get onto her, "If Lenox spoke to me the way you spoke to me, Mr Napier would not have that. He'd be down on him like a ton of bricks. I

51

said they all had to have respect for me as what I had for them. You don't want to worry about that." And then one day she give me a list of things to do from here to here, and wanted me to do that in a day. I thought to myself she was taking the mickey of me. I said to the woman what did work for her, "I'm not going to take this. I'm coming in Wednesday but I'm not going to come no more." Johnny and Pat come to pick me up and bring me over to Hingham on the Saturday. I was going to have a fortnight holiday, and then I was going back home but I didn't go back no more.

T: How long did you work for Mrs Matthews?

J: Not very long, about three weeks, that was quite long enough. As I told you, I left the Napiers on the Monday. The Tuesday she was there at our door. And I said to her, "I'm going to take three months off work." She knew that because I'd already got that sorted out with the dole people.

T: She was very bossy?

J: Not much she wasn't. If she told you to go out there and cut that lawn, it was no good your saying it's too wet, because if she told you to do it, you'd have to do it.

T: And that was quite different from the Napiers?

J: Cor, not much. I said to her once because Lenox went there to school, "Was Lenox good?" She said, "What's it got to do with you what Lenox done there?" I didn't think there was any harm; all she had to say was yes or no. I didn't like that because the Napiers were my life. So I wasn't going to work for her. Johnny said I'm going to phone up Mrs Matthews. I said it really should be me who phone, but he spoke to her, and told me, "I nearly said yes, you can go and work for her, but I knew you didn't want to go and had a job to explain to her that you wouldn't." I went along church once, and she was there. She kept shouting, "Joan let me down," and I said I didn't. In a way she let me down, because she come after me when Mum and Dad were both dying. Dad only had a month to live even though he committed suicide. But Mum would have gone first because she was

52

definitely going to go that weekend. The doctor told me that.

T: You lost your Mum and Dad, you lost the job at the Napiers, you might have thought that this is awful, but that's partly the effect of grieving, isn't it?

J: I think so. I felt that because Mrs Matthews was so pushy, I never did grieve for my parents, honestly speaking. It wasn't just leaving them, it was a whole way of life, gone.

T: That was cruel of her.

J: She didn't think to realise what was going on. I went to see Mrs Howard to tell her that Mum was dying. She was at Rawhall, where Mum used to bike or walk. If she got a puncture, she used to walk then, until Dad mended the puncture, or Johnny, or one on them, so she used to walk up there, or walk off home. It was quite a long way.

Mum worked for the Howards so I went and told Mrs Howard that the Napiers were away, and I thought to myself that Michelle, her daughter, was going to come off home and I thought I'll give her a helping hand and then I can tell her that Mum is on the way out. I didn't want Mrs Howard to find her dead and think she was responsible if you see what I'm meaning. If I could tell her she's dying then she would know it had nothing to do with her, because I said to her you can't stop Mum from coming here because that would be cruel, because she would not understand what she'd done wrong. So Mrs Howard got up there on the Friday morning and Mum said, "I'm going to work for Mrs Howard today." Well of course that's when she died, you see. She didn't get that far.

My brother Tony worked for Mrs Howard a little while and then he went to the Andrews for a little. He sort of like had one or two jobs. I felt sorry for Tony because he was seventeen, and that's an awkward stage in life. But he went to live along of Olive and Geoff in Gressenhall. Geoffrey wanted him there so I let him go.

T: It must have been difficult for both of you, being that young.

Ghost at Bittering Hall

Now I come to tell you what happened to me with the policeman. One day when the Napiers were away, their dog came and met me, that was Tensing, a damn great dog – an African hound – he came and met me, Tensing did. That's his name after the man what went up to the top of Everest. It was an unusual name! Anyway, I'd been up to the Hall to make sure everything was alright and the dog never come and met me before. That didn't bark, that didn't do anything.

T: Was it about the same size as you?

J: Yes! Children used to ride on its back, like a donkey! That's a lovable dog, don't get me wrong but it was huge. It came and met me, and I went up the drive and I could hear this banging round in the old part of the Hall, and I was going in what we call the new part because they had the kitchen moved from the old part into the new part, but they kept the old kitchen as an old kitchen, because they let that part of the Hall. There was this here "bang, bang, bang." I went inside the hall, and I thought, "That's something odd, I'll have to phone the police." So I phoned the police and told them to come up the front drive, not go up the back drive. The policeman was getting out of the car, and I said to him, "You can hear the banging."

T: Did you think someone had broken in?

J: Yes, I mean there was no one there. The policeman came and said, "I had better phone for back-up," because we could hear the banging, we both could hear it. But when that come to it, there wasn't a mark on the door, there weren't anything at all. The only proof I had that I could hear the banging was the policeman could hear as well as me. And we checked all the cupboards, all the wardrobes in case it was anyone inside, but there was nothing, nowhere. The other policeman said to me, "You got us here on a fool's errand." No, the first policeman said, "I heard it, she heard it." And I thought that the way there was banging, there was more than one person. There wasn't a mark on the door, there wasn't a mark on the windowsill, there wasn't a mark nowhere.

T: So this is the ghost, is it?

J: That's what we put it down to. But I tell you another thing. On the day I left the Hall, after the Napiers had gone, they left me to lock up, and I had to put the Hall keys into the stable flats. Do you know what? There was a different atmosphere in that Hall, I can't explain it, it just came over me before I went out. That didn't frighten me, but I thought to myself, "Thank the Lord, I'm out of here for good."

T: The Napiers had gone to Spain by this time?

J: They were on their way. They were going down to the dairy to say cheerio to the man in the dairy, and then they were going to Spain. I was there for about half an hour or more after they were gone, but the atmosphere just changed, I'll never forget it. I can't explain it, do you know what I mean? Because there was no one there, only me. I was always on me own. I never felt lonely because I had Mum and Dad at home, and also I had my work. I used to go out with the Napiers a time or two. I never felt isolated, if that's the word to use.

LEAVING BITTERING

T: When your mother and father died you went and lived with your sister Margaret.

J: In Beeston. About three months I should say.

T: Your Mum died in June and that's when you went to Beeston?

J: I didn't start work at Mackintosh's [in Norwich] until the 2nd October. I knew I was going to start there on my birthday. That is when I made a start but I couldn't make a start till someone leave. I mean I wouldn't take anyone else's job. That isn't fair. But once I knew there was a job there, I took it, you know.

I could have stayed there in Bittering, there was nothing to stop me, but the fact was I was being harassed by other people. Will you come here? Will you come there? I felt that if I was an animal, they'd pick the bones off of me, and leave me the bones while they took the flesh, because they took after me like anything. I could have went to work in Beeston, went to work for the Howards, I could've went to work for Mrs Matthews, and I didn't want to work for any of them.

You see, how I come to go off Norwich was, I went to the Norwood Rooms from the Napiers, to a party there. And there were two men there, one was Mr Clarke who used to run the Norwood Rooms [when the Capitol Cinema in Norwich was closed in April 1960, it was converted into the Lido Ballroom, later known as the Norwood Rooms]. And there was someone else, a chef. They both offered me a job in Norwich because they knew the Napiers were leaving. I didn't know! They were the first ones who told me. And they said to me, "Do you realise they are going to Spain?" First of all, I said no I didn't know, for goodness sake, don't put the wind up on me tonight, sort of thing. But I got offered two jobs. The other one said I could work part-time in the canteen at Mackintosh's, and the other job was full-time at Laurence and Scott. Just after the party in January 1966, Mr Clarke came to the Hall. He had spilt wine over Mrs Napier's dress at a party there and he wanted to pay for the cleaning. There was no one in but me. I was upset because the doctor had just said Mum and Dad were dying, so I wanted to get away, but I did tell him that I wanted to go to Hingham and live along of John and Pat. He said, "Come and work for me at Laurence and Scott." He never did pay the money for the cleaning!

So when I come to Hingham, I already got jobs, so I never been out of work, if you know what I mean.

One door closes and one opens. For me, your life's just planned from the time you're born until the time you die but you can't see what's going on in the middle of it. Who'd have thought at Bittering I'd get offered two jobs at Norwich. It seems impossible.

Whatever happen is, we were always brought up in a religious family, as far as that go, I hent saying they rose to the top, but I always think, like Dad used to say, God provide us with the food for the table. Instead of saying thank you God for what we are about to receive, we always had to thank Him for the food what He provided. And if you think of it, He did. Who made the rabbits? He made the hares. Who made the wildlife? I know we got to look after it.

Going to Mackintosh's, then Laurence and Scott in Norwich

[Mackintosh's was the sweet factory in Norwich formed from Caley's, which was established in the late nineteenth century and sold to John Mackintosh and Son Ltd in 1932. It was taken over by Rowntrees in 1969 to form Rowntree Mackintosh (and has subsequently closed). Laurence and Scott was set up in Norwich at the end of the nineteenth century to make electric motors and dynamos; in 1929 it took over Electromotors. When Joan was working in the canteen from late 1967 to December 1968, it continued to make electric motors and other electrical apparatus.]

J: I went to Mackintosh's for part-time work first before I went to Laurence and Scott. I was only there about a couple of months. It was no good to me, part-time work, being single. But then at the same time I learnt a lot while I was there, how the canteen was run, and that would have been too much for me to go there full-time, 'cos the air was different, and the noises, all those lorries. I'd never been used to all that noise, and the amount of people. But I learnt a lot while I was there and that got me ready to work at Laurence and Scott full-time. I was lucky, that's all I can say.

T: Although it was a special part of your life being brought up in Bittering and working at the Hall there, in a way it was good for you to see Norwich, and work in Norwich, wasn't it?

J: I hated it. When I first went there, to Laurence and Scott, I went up the Thorpe Road and I seed this here chicken netting over the windows on wooden frames – you opened the window and then you have to push the net back. That was against a bomb or anything like that, then it wouldn't shatter the windows.

T: During the war, you mean?

J: And after. We had the wire up there when I worked there. That was one of the things that I thought, "Strewth, where have I come to? I fell off the biggest blooming Christmas tree." I had worked for decent people, and my bloomin' heart went through the floor. Where the hell had I come to? I had no idea. I didn't expect it, coming from the country up to the city.

T: Did it get better as you worked there?

J: Yes. When Joan Wortley walked through the door at Laurence and Scott, I was alright then. We were just country people, working together, and we hit it off straight away. Like I told you before, in somewhere like Bittering, you don't grow up so much as what you do in the city or even here in Hingham 'cos life is so much different.

I don't think I could have stuck Laurence and Scott straightaway. The thing on it is, at Mackintosh's everything was more updated. You didn't get netting over the windows. You can see through them. It just felt like a school canteen, but in the bigger sense. But when I went to Laurence and Scott, that was different altogether. When you worked in the canteen in the offices, all you got was little slits in the wall, that's all you could see outside. You push them one way and you can just see through the gap. There were hardly any windows. I had worked down in the canteen, and it was nice just to see the sky, but you couldn't stand all day out there. One day I stood there looking at the building, and the man said, "What are you looking at?" I said, "That bit there is sort of like creamy, and that there . . ." He said that was done like that so that when the Germans came over, they couldn't see where Laurence and Scott was. That's all camouflage for them. That's something what I never give a thought about.

T: So the camouflage was still all there?

J: Yeah. When I went there.

It was a lot to take in. I'm not saying I was unhappy there because I wasn't, but you think to yourself why have I come here?

T: Was the pay at Laurence and Scott better then you were getting at the Hall?

J: Yes, it was. A lot better. But I didn't go for the pay. As long as I

58

got a pound in my pocket I couldn't care less, you know. There's a lot to be thankful for than just money. I wouldn't like to be without money, well I never have been.

Anyway, I never regretted it, and I never regretted being at Norwich. I was glad when I talked them [Laurence and Scott] into doing the survey about the canteen and putting it in the company newspaper because to me that is no longer there, that's all history. But when you think about being in Bittering and then to go up to Laurence and Scott there's no comparison, no one in-between, is there? One extreme to the other. But it is in this country, that's not in Spain.

Moving to Hingham

When I came to them when Pat and John got married, I stayed with her aunt up Fleeters Hill, and I said to her that I wouldn't mind coming to live in Hingham, but I don't think I ever shall. We didn't go far, but we just went around town like you do and I got the feeling of Hingham and said I wouldn't mind coming to live here.

I came and lived with John and Pat for six and a half years in 1967. After Mum and Dad died I went to Hingham for a rest. I knew I was tired. But I never went back. [In 1968 Joan was told she had rheumatoid arthritis, which hit her fully when she was 58 (in year 2000) and she had to stop work.]

I started work at Norwich on my birthday, 2nd October 1967. I got a council bungalow when I got married in 1973. We got the house [in Greenacre Road] on 8th December, and we got married on the 23rd! Georgie, my husband, had lived in Hingham all his life.

T: You took the bus in to Norwich?

J: Yes. Till I met Georgie. He gave me a lift in his car.

T: Where did you live in Hingham for the first six years?

J: I was in Glebe Close most part of the time in a private bungalow. Till I got married, some of the time I lived with Georgie's Mum and Dad in the bungalow, because they moved out, then they went back. But the whole time I was here at Hingham, as far as the council was concerned I was always there at Glebe Close. I spent most of my time there till I got married. Then I come here.

When Mum and Dad died, Tony went and lived along with my oldest sister Olive, he went there to Gressenhall, and I came this way because I got jobs up in Norwich, so that split the family. He went and lived along with Geoffrey and Olive and I came this way with John and Pat.

T: Is Margaret still alive?

J: She's up in Scotland now. Just Johnny and Olive have gone.

T: How does Margaret remember her childhood?

J: She said we could have spent more time in Longham. But she didn't say we didn't have a good childhood. I think in a way she's a factory girl, who would like to have had more out of life. But with me I was quite happy just being around Bittering. I'm quite happy with Bittering now!

T: And where is Tony?

J: He's now at North Elmham, along with his wife Gloria.

Living in Hingham

Here in Hingham that's just cushy. I mean, I got a lot of work on the house done when Georgie was ill. That had to be done because if I ended up with a chill, or if I did housework again, I'd have such a job getting these things. So if you've got them, just hang onto them because that's such a rigmarole. There again that's all bloomin' paperwork. The paperwork is what takes the time. It isn't getting these things, it's not getting the paperwork done.

I do like living here. I did want this bungalow. I wanted it more than what Georgie did, I must agree on that. To get this, if that had been an organ, there wouldn't be one stop what wouldn't be pulled out! I couldn't have done no more. When I got it I was pleased.

60

T: It is compact, warm, in good condition, green, quiet.

J: I couldn't live in a better place than Hingham, I always said I liked living in Hingham, I hent saying I didn't. I get on well with Hingham people. They're friendly and that like. Especially since George been gone. I go to church and do different things, more than what I would have done elsewhere.

I've now started going to the Nattering Knitting. I don't knit but I natter. There hent hardly anyone there what do any knitting.

That's funny how life really turn out. There is so much going on here. Take the Queen's Birthday Party. I wouldn't have had that in Bittering.

When I came here in a way I was getting Norfolk, but I hated that up Norwich, it took me a couple of years before I settled down. As far as I was concerned, I was working and that was it. I couldn't give in to my feelings that I wanted to go off home. I did get homesick, I must agree. Because like I said before if I had met Georgie when I was down at Bittering, probably things would have been a lot different.

Meeting George

T: It was at Laurence and Scott that you first met George?

J: Yeah, in 1967, and we started going out in 1968. I met him over the river.

T: Did he give you a wave?

J: I used to go down there 'cos I didn't have nothing in common with the women. They used to talk about nightclubs! To me that was all foreign. I didn't know the half of what they were talking about, I didn't honestly. So I used to go down to the river. There was an old boy down there, he was the harbourmaster. And he knew more about Norwich and the river Wensum than anybody. I used to talk to him, and Georgie was over the other side. We used to shout at each other, and when I finished my dinner, I used to feed the seagulls. The first thing George ever said to me was, "Stop feeding them bloody seagulls because they keep shitting on my car and taking the colour off." Then the harbourmaster shouted to him, and that's how we came to go out together.

T: That's a nice story. George had been in the Navy during the war. Where was he working when you met?

J: He was at Colman's when I first met him.

T: He lived in Hingham, didn't he?

J: Yeah. 15 Baxter Road.

T: How long has Georgie been gone now?

J: Three years come January. Don't seem that long, that don't.

T: He was older than you, wasn't he?

J: Yes. There were seventeen years between us. That never did make any difference to me, nor to him either come to that. Certainly not to me. We got on alright. He was always there, that's the thing. I hent saying we had an easy marriage, because we didn't. Not really, because things were difficult with his Mum. The thing on it was, what I felt sorry for her was, she lived in Baxter Row, where the garages are. They stand well back. That used to be two cottages there. Well, they used to be a shop, and then they turned it into two cottages. Georgie's Mum lived on one side, and his Dad, and in the other side was his brother, so there were two brothers living side-by-side. Well they got evicted out of there, so they went into 15 Baxter Row, and George and his Mum went into 15 Lincoln Close. Then the farm wanted her and George out. We got this house on 8th December 1973, and she got her notice on 4th January 1974. So she had to get out and the following week that was on Tuesday 11th January when the bailiffs come round. I was round there cleaning up in the garage. The bailiffs turned up and said we'd got to evict Georgie's Mum and Georgie, and I said to them, "She's already gone." "Gone, where she gone?" I said she's gone into a one-bedroomed bungalow. I said she went on Saturday. He said, "We know she was an eighty-year-old woman, so we have got to be careful how we do it." I said, "She's gone and her son has gone. He's staying along with me." Anyhow, they were going to give me the paperwork, like how they do, and they see all this rubbish, and I think they felt a bit sorry for her. I said I got to take all this rubbish up to Greenacre Road. Well anyhow, they poured that in the back of the van and Joanie here weren't going to walk off home because I had just about had it. So I got in the back of the van with all the rubbish and I hurt my backside on the rubbish! I don't know what was pricking into me but I couldn't say, "Will you stop, I want to get out!"

T: So they took you down here and you unloaded?

J: They unloaded me and the rubbish, and then they came in and I said to them – I wasn't on the phone then – can you get in touch with the Council and they got Mr Jones on the phone, and he came round at Laurence and Scott, and we done all the paperwork there in a car by the railway lines. My boss thought that was Georgie in there, and wondered what was going on. I said, "No, this is the Council bloke with the paperwork, and I couldn't have the Tuesday off, so we done the business in the car."

But I did feel sorry for Georgie's Mum. They evicted her twice out the same street, and I assure you she didn't want to go. She really didn't. She said to the farmer, "I'm sitting on my chair," and she was a strong-willed woman, but she said, "I'm sitting on my chair, and you got to take me out on my chair." Well, she nearly did that, but she did walk out. Imagine her sitting on top of the chair getting on top of the trailer! That's like the hillbillies! She'd been evicted twice, from the same street, and she had lived in the street ever since she'd been married, and then all of a sudden she's in her eighties and she's chucked out in the same street. You can't help feeling sorry for her.

BITTERING TODAY

Demolition of the Hall

J: Lenox was heartbroken when he knew that was being demolished. He thought, "That's my home and they're knocking it down."

T: Someone bought it off the Napiers?

J: That was the Leggatts that bought it off them. I think they tried to make money more than anything. They said that was noisy from the stone pits [the aggregate extraction in the quarries at Bittering], and that might have been. That was half on it. There was two families. I think the older Leggatts, his Mum and Dad, had one half, and they had the other half, what they could easily do because it was already in flats.

T: It's a bit drastic to knock it down though. Was it leaking?

J: I always said the roof wanted doing. I said that when the Napiers were there. I even told Lenox there. I said, "Really and truly, Lenox, it want a lot of money spent on it." When that rained, sometime the water used to come through the ceiling. I said not only that, it all want new wiring, new plugs and everything, the front hall all want decorating. He said, "You are right." Otherwise his Mum and Dad would never have done what they'd done. I tried him round in their way of thinking. I didn't want Lenox to think badly of what they'd done. I was really fond of them.

*

Bittering hent bombed down, but it fell down. Every time you go back there, there's something disappearing. You're looking for it. You have an idea where it is but it's not there.

T: Would you like to see some new houses built at Bittering?

J: Well, people won't want to live there, would they?

T: Too far away?

64

J: Yes. They have made some of the barns into houses and that, like, and people live there. I can't see them ever building there. I mean, a long while ago in the sixties, they built bungalows there at Longham. But it was a hard job just to get them done, even in Longham. They built some in Beeston, but they hent built any more. These were council houses. I hent saying they aren't needed, but then people today like to go to towns and they like to be near towns, they don't like to live out in the sticks.

T: They want the services.

J: There is everything at Litcham. A doctor's, the shop, the school, butcher's. There was a garage, but whether it's still there I don't know. So you had communities there.

T: Hingham is quite well provided.

J: That's right.

*

J: What did <u>you</u> think of Bittering?

T: It felt so remote, although it's not in fact remote because there are other villages nearby. When I had first walked through the parish, on one of our long walks, I knew you had come from Bittering, and we found a little parish church, not much else. I walked past your house without knowing it had been your house, of course. It was like those Norfolk villages – there's a house here and a house there, it's a village but it's not a village. Not like Hingham with a group of houses round the village green.

J: I did enjoy living around Bittering, but I wouldn't want to go back as the work isn't there. The Hall is gone. Bell Hall is gone, and a lot of the cottages are gone. What would I actually do round there? But I never regret the life I had. I have been abroad for a weekend, that's all, but I feel I've done a lot in my life.

ANNEXES

1: THE CATHOLIC CHAPEL IN BITTERING

Norfolk has a number of hidden churches, but the chapel at Bittering is one of the most secret. It is a Catholic shrine dedicated to the Virgin Mary, and although Norfolk churches are examples if not of eternity then at least of longevity, this chapel, only dedicated in 1975, is already beginning to be lost among the leaves and trunks of the wood.

However, the story behind it is remarkable. It was built, almost single-handedly, by Paul Hodác, a young man when the Nazis invaded Czechoslovakia. He joined in its defence, but in vain. He escaped to Poland: "It was very difficult and dangerous but I managed it all right. I relied on nobody but myself." Then from Poland, invaded in its turn, he went to Romania, then Beirut, then France. When France in its turn fell, he came to Britain and finally found a refuge from Nazism.

He discovered Norfolk on holiday, spending time in Bittering from the early 1960s. He bought Spread Oak Wood so that he could build a shrine to the Virgin Mary as a token of thanks for his escape, and also to honour the Czech airmen who were based at Wretham airfield in the south-west of Norfolk.

The result is this humble but moving shrine.

(Note: the full story can be read in the Eastern Daily Press for Saturday 27 January 2001. It is also referred to in 'The Book of Wendling, Longham and Beeston with Bittering' by Stephen Olley, Hallsgrove 2005.)

2: THE NAPIER FAMILY TREE

The Napier family has a connection with William Wilberforce (1759-1833), the prominent campaigner for the abolition of the slave trade. In the Kelly's Directory entry of 1937 for Bittering, one of the residents is listed as the Reverend RW Puleston of Bittering Hall. Puleston was a great-grandson of William Wilberforce (and grandson of Samuel Wilberforce, successively Bishop of Oxford and Winchester) whose surname derives from that of his wife Catherine TF Puleston, lady of the manor. Reginald Puleston was a 'squarson' or 'squire parson' as rector of St Peter and St Paul Bittering for fifty years. Catherine died in 1942 but curiously the date of his death is elusive, nor is it recorded on the Wilberforce Family Tree website (www.wilberforce.info/index.htm) .

Reginald and Catherine had a daughter Barbara who died in 1926, aged twenty-six, but not before she had given birth to William Puleston Scott Napier. It was William and Heather Napier's family, and their son Lenox, whom Joan worked for in Bittering Hall.

This is yet another case of Bittering being home to a vanishing piece of British history. The story as a whole presents a picture of a family with a distinguished name from before the First World War carrying on well into the twentieth century, the squarson giving way to the family in the big house, gradually shedding its servants and moving to Spain in 1967. Heather Napier died in 1978 and William in 1986. There is a plaque to each of them in the parish church.

3: WENDLING AIRFIELD

Joan was very young during the war but the presence of Wendling airfield just south of Bittering was an important part of Bittering memory in her childhood. It was used by the USAAF Eighth Air Force ('the Mighty Eighth') to fly 285 missions in B-24 Liberators, but by the end of May 1945 it was relinquished to return to farmland. Some of the tracks through Honeypot Wood, a Norfolk Wildlife Trust reserve, must have been part of the airfield but the main runways are now beneath a field of corn.

SFORZINDA BOOKS

Sforzinda Books is the outlet for the publishing of Tim Cawkwell. He is the author of several books on film, travel and cricket:

- *The World Encyclopaedia of Film* (co-editor, 1972)
- *Film Past Film Future* (2011)
- *Temenos 2012*, a diary about the Temenos film festival in Greece in 2012
- *From Neuralgistan to the Elated Kingdom: a personal journey inside Sicily* (2013)
- *Between Wee Free and Wi Fi: Scotland and the UK belong surely?* (2013)
- *The New Filmgoer's Guide to God* (2014)
- *A Tivoli Companion* (2015)
- *Cricket's Pure Pleasure: the story of an extraordinary match – Middlesex v. Yorkshire, September 2015* (2016)
- *The Tale of Two Terriers and the Somerset Cat: the County Championship 2016* (2017)
- *Belaboured. Bats Broken. Britain Shaken – a personal account of the 2017 General Election* (2017).
- *Compleat Cricket: eight days in September* (2018).

In 2008 he launched his own website for writing about the cinema, www.timcawkwell.co.uk, later adding to it a Wordpress blog, www.cawkwell200.com. His dvd LIGHT YEARS: THE FILM DIARIES OF TIM CAWKWELL 1968 TO 1987 was released in 2018.

He was born in 1948 and lives in Norwich in the United Kingdom.

Printed in Great Britain
by Amazon